THANK YOU, EARTHWORMS

BY EMMA HUDDLESTON

Published by The Child's World®
1980 Lookout Drive • Mankato, MN 56003-1705
800-599-READ • www.childsworld.com

Photographs ©: Andrei Metelev/Shutterstock Images, cover, 1; Shutterstock Images, 2, 13 (soil), 13 (worms), 14, 21, 24; iStockphoto, 5; Witaya Proadtayakogool/Shutterstock Images, 6, 10; Mark Baldwin/Shutterstock Images, 9; Orest lyzhechka/Shutterstock Images, 17; Krit Leoniz/Shutterstock Images, 18

Copyright © 2022 by The Child's World®
All rights reserved. No part of this book may be reproduced or utilized in any form or by any means without written permission from the publisher.

ISBN 9781503849976 (Reinforced Library Binding)
ISBN 9781503850477 (Portable Document Format)
ISBN 9781503851238 (Online Multi-user eBook)
LCCN 2021939875

Printed in the United States of America

ABOUT THE AUTHOR

Emma Huddleston lives in Minnesota with her husband. She enjoys running, swing dancing, and writing books for young readers.

TABLE OF CONTENTS

CHAPTER ONE
From the Ground Up ...4

CHAPTER TWO
Keeping the Soil Healthy ...11

CHAPTER THREE
Life without Earthworms ...16

GLOSSARY ...22
TO LEARN MORE ...23
INDEX ...24

From the Ground Up

A reddish-brown earthworm crawls out of its tunnel. It moves across the soil. It has a long, skinny body. It wriggles through fallen leaves and dead grass. Its body is made of ringed **segments**. Each part has small hairs. The worms use these hairs to grip the ground and move.

Earthworms can be many colors. Most are pink or reddish, but they can also be gray or brown.

Earthworms eat plant matter and animal waste. This process returns nutrients to the soil.

The earthworm eats a leaf. By eating leaves off the ground, the worm is cleaning up. This helps get rid of scraps on the ground. The earthworm is also recycling. It recycles plant matter's **nutrients** through its waste. This helps plants grow. Scraps are broken up inside the worm's body and then expelled as waste. Bacteria and smaller **organisms** can use the waste for food.

Earthworms keep the soil healthy. Healthy soil helps plants grow. Plants provide food for animals and people. Earthworms help the soil by breaking down dead matter and mixing up soil layers. Healthy soil makes for a healthy ecosystem. An ecosystem is the environment and all plants and animals that live there.

FUN FACT

Earthworms are also called night crawlers. They get that name because they often come above ground at night to eat.

Many ecosystems rely on earthworms for healthy soil.

Most worms are active during the daytime. Worms often stay near the surface.

Keeping the Soil Healthy

Earthworms improve soil by wriggling through it. They break the soil apart and make it loose. When soil is loose, air and water can move through it more easily. Water helps plants grow. Loose soil also makes it easier for plant roots to spread out and find nutrients.

Most earthworms are a few inches long. But some grow to be more than 14 inches (36 cm).

Land may suffer from floods. Flooding can wash away soil and seeds. Then the seeds won't grow. When soil has earthworms living in it, it is able to **absorb** rain better than in places without these animals. This helps areas avoid flooding. Tunnels and holes in the dirt let water **seep** down. Soil holds water. Some earthworms can dig up to 6.5 feet (2 m) down. Digging deep helps the soil hold more water.

Types of Earthworms

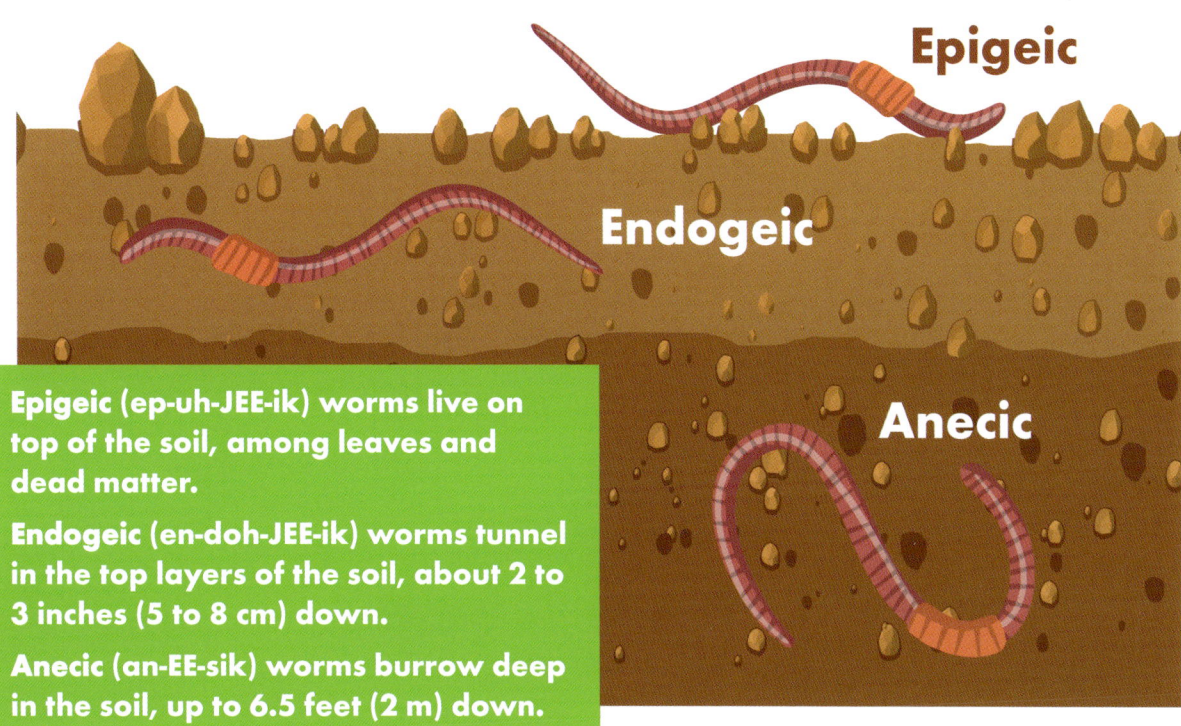

Epigeic (ep-uh-JEE-ik) worms live on top of the soil, among leaves and dead matter.

Endogeic (en-doh-JEE-ik) worms tunnel in the top layers of the soil, about 2 to 3 inches (5 to 8 cm) down.

Anecic (an-EE-sik) worms burrow deep in the soil, up to 6.5 feet (2 m) down.

Worms live in all parts of the soil. They share many of the same jobs. All three types of worms break down plant matter. Both endogeic and anecic worms tunnel through the soil.

There may be as many as one million earthworms in 1 acre (.4 hectares) of healthy soil.

Healthy soil helps plants and people. For example, grass grows better and faster in soils with earthworms. Farmers use grass to feed cows. More grass means they can raise more cows. Cows provide milk and meat for people around the world. Healthy soil is also helpful for **crop** growth. Crops such as corn are major food sources for people.

Earthworms are also food for many animals. Birds, frogs, toads, and racoons find worms above ground. Bugs, snakes, mice, and moles find worms underground.

Life without Earthworms

Earthworms are threatened by some farming activities. Farmers use machines to break up soil and get rid of weeds. This creates clean and dry fields. But this is bad for worms. Worms need some water in the soil. No weeds also means less food for the worms. The machines can kill earthworms, too. Some **fertilizers** also harm earthworms. Fertilizers are used to help plants grow. But they can kill creatures such as worms.

Many farmers use machines to break up soil in their fields. This process is called tilling.

Some people use worms to break down food scraps at home. They can use the worm waste to help the soil in their gardens.

Without earthworms, matter would pile up. In forests, dead plants could start to add up. In fields, animal waste might build up. If this happens, soil would suffer. That could cause problems for plant health. Eventually, people may not have enough crops to eat. Also, several types of animals eat earthworms. These animals need earthworms to survive. There would also be a lack of healthy soil and plants without earthworms. This would mean less food for other animals to eat as well.

More than 7,000 **species** of earthworms exist. They live in many types of soil. Wet and warm places are best for worms. It is difficult for worms to live in cold or dry ground. Earthworms live all around the world. They help ecosystems thrive.

FUN FACT

Baby worms hatch from cocoons. These cocoons are smaller than a grain of rice.

There are more than 180 types of earthworms in the United States and Canada.

absorb (ab-SORB) To absorb is to take in. Loose soil will absorb the water from rain.

cocoons (kuh-KOONZ) Cocoons are silk coverings that protect certain small animals or their eggs. Baby worms hatch from cocoons.

crop (KRAHP) A crop is a plant that is a major food source for people. Corn is an important crop.

fertilizers (FUR-tuh-ly-zurz) Fertilizers are substances used to help plants grow. Fertilizers can harm soil and earthworms that live there.

nutrients (NOO-tree-uhnts) Nutrients are substances found in food that help living things grow. Worms recycle nutrients in their waste.

organisms (OR-guh-nih-zuhms) Organisms are life-forms, including all plants and animals. Many organisms live in soil.

seep (SEEP) To seep is to soak into. Over time, water will seep into soil.

segments (SEG-mentz) Segments are different parts of an object marked off by lines. An earthworm's body has segments.

species (SPEE-sheez) A species is a specific group of animals that has the same features. Thousands of earthworm species exist.

BOOKS

Huddleston, Emma. *Looking into Soil.* Mankato, MN: The Child's World, 2020.

Patterson, Jack K. *Worms.* New York, NY: Cavendish Square, 2019.

Williams, Susie. *Worms.* New York, NY: Crabtree Publishing, 2020.

WEBSITES

Visit our website for links about earthworms:
childsworld.com/links

Note to Parents, Teachers, and Librarians: We routinely verify our Web links to make sure they are safe and active sites. So encourage your readers to check them out!

INDEX

bacteria, 7

crops, 15, 19

fertilizers, 16

hairs, 4

leaves, 4–7, 13

night crawlers, 8
nutrients, 7, 11

organisms, 7

segments, 4
soil, 4, 8, 11–12, 13, 15, 16, 19–20
species, 20

tunnels, 4, 12, 13

waste, 7, 19